Learning to Write
Adjectives

WEIGL PUBLISHERS INC.

Published by Weigl Publishers Inc.
350 5th Avenue, Suite 3304, PMB 6G
New York, NY 10118-0069

Website: www.weigl.com
Copyright ©2010 WEIGL PUBLISHERS INC.

All of the Internet URLs given in the book were valid at the time of publication. However, due to the
dynamic nature of the Internet, some addresses may have changed, or sites may have ceased to exist
since publication. While the author and publisher regret any inconvenience this may cause readers,
no responsibility for any such changes can be accepted by either the author or the publisher.

Library of Congress Cataloging-in-Publication Data

Lambert, Deborah.
 Adjectives / Deborah Lambert.
    p. cm. -- (Learning to write)
 Includes webliography and index.
 ISBN 978-1-60596-048-7 (hard cover : alk. paper) -- ISBN 978-1-60596-049-4 (soft cover : alk.
paper)
 1. English language--adjective--Juvenile literature. I. Title.
 PE1241.L36 2009
 428.2--dc22

                              2009001954

Printed in China
1 2 3 4 5 6 7 8 9 0 13 12 11 10 09

Editor: Deborah G. Lambert
Design: Terry Paulhus

Photograph Credits

Weigl acknowledges Shutterstock, iStockphoto, and Dreamstime as the primary image suppliers for
this title. Unless otherwise noted, all images herein were obtained from Shutterstock, iStockphoto,
Dreamstime and their contributors.

All of the internet URLs given in the book were valid at the time of publication. However, due to the
dynamic nature of the internet, some addresses may have changed, or sites may have ceased to exist
since publication. While the author and publisher regret any inconvenience this may cause readers,
no responsibility for any such changes can be accepted by either the author or the publisher.

Every reasonable effort has been made to trace ownership and to obtain permission to reprint
copyright material. The publishers would be pleased to have any errors or omissions brought
to their attention so that they may be corrected in subsequent printings.

Table of Contents

Table of Contents

What is an Adjective?

An adjective is a part of speech that tells something about a **noun** or **pronoun**. It usually describes *which, what kind,* or *how many.*

An adjective helps us to picture a noun or pronoun more clearly. Most times, an adjective is placed before the noun or pronoun. Sometimes, it may come after a **being verb**.

Examples of adjectives are shaded red in this paragraph about one of the regions in the United States.

The South is made up of 16 states. It is known for its warm weather. In the past, cotton, tobacco, rice, and sugarcane were important crops in the South. They shaped southern history. More than 100 million people live in the South. Many people of African, Hispanic, and European backgrounds live there. Together, southerners share a special history and culture. Well-known writers, such as Tennessee Williams, have lived there.

To read more about the South, go to **www.factmonster.com/ipka/A0875011.html**. Look for examples of adjectives being used to describe the rich history of the South.

Finding the Adjectives

The following paragraph tells a story about Hawai'i's yellow hibiscus flower. The words "hibiscus" and "yellow" describe the flower.

*The hibiscus flower is the **symbol** of Hawai'i. This yellow flower became Hawai'i's state flower in 1988. It is a tropical flower that grows naturally on six out of eight of the main islands. Once, the hibiscus grew on all of the Hawai'ian Islands. Today, it is **endangered**. Only about 60 hibiscus plants still live in nature.*

Try to find other adjectives in this paragraph. How many did you find? Now study the picture of the hibiscus flower. In your notebook, write down three other adjectives that you think describe this flower.

Identifying Types of Adjectives

There are many types of adjectives. Here is a list of some of these adjectives and what they do to nouns or pronouns.

- **Descriptive adjectives** describe the size, color, and quality of nouns or pronouns
- **Comparative adjectives** compare nouns or pronouns
- **Adjectives that tell** *which* point to a particular noun or pronoun
- **Adjectives that tell** *how many* show the amount or number of nouns or pronouns
- **Articles,** such as *a* and *an* point to any noun or pronoun, and *the* points to a particular noun or pronoun

Examples of some of these types of adjectives have been shaded red in this paragraph about Missouri's flowering dogwood. Try writing the paragraph without these adjectives, and read it aloud. How do the adjectives make the sentences more clear?

The flowering dogwood is a beautiful tree that became Missouri's state tree in 1955. In spring, tiny clusters of yellowish flowers stay in bloom for about three weeks. These are surrounded by four large white or pink leaves. In the fall, the tree's leaves turn bright red, orange, or purple. Red berries dot the tree.

Selecting Types of Adjectives

These paragraphs describe the state **seals** of Ohio and Maine. Find the adjectives in the paragraphs, and list them in your notebook.

Ohio's seal portrays the state's landscapes. The Sun radiates over Mount Logan in the background. The Scioto River separates the mountain from flat fields of wheat. Thirteen rays of Sun symbolize America's 13 original colonies, while the wheat shows the importance of agriculture. A bundle of 17 arrows represents Ohio as the 17th state to join the Union. Ohio's current seal was adopted in 1996.

Maine's seal was adopted in 1820. This was the same year Maine achieved statehood. Symbols on the seal represent the natural beauty, resources, and industry in Maine. On the shield, a moose rests under a pine tree. A farmer and a sailor stand on either side of the shield. The North star is at the top of the seal, with the motto Dirigo underneath. This means "I lead."

What did you learn about the state seals of Ohio and Maine? Visit **www.netstate.com/state_seals.htm** to learn about the seals of the other states. Look for the adjectives in these descriptions, and add them to your list.

Learning about Descriptive Adjectives

Descriptive adjectives describe the size, color, and quality of nouns or pronouns. To describe means to make a picture with words or give more details about a noun or pronoun.

Descriptive adjectives are used in this paragraph about the Minnesota red pine. These adjectives are shaded red.

The red pine is named for the tree's reddish-brown bark. It has long needles that snap when bent. Red pines can survive harsh weather and bad soil. Birds, such as bald eagles, nest in them. The red pine became Minnesota's state tree in 1945. The tallest red pine in Minnesota is 126 feet tall and more than 300 years old.

In the paragraph, the adjectives "red" and "reddish-brown" give details about the color of the Minnesota red pine. The adjectives "long" and "tallest" give details about the pine's needles and height. "Harsh," "bad," and "bald" give details about the quality of the **environment** in which the pine grows. These adjectives help you to picture the Minnesota pine clearly.

Identifying Descriptive Adjectives

The following paragraphs describe the state birds of Oklahoma and Virginia. Read the paragraphs, and in your notebook, write a list of all the descriptive adjectives.

Oklahoma's state bird is the scissor-tailed flycatcher. This is a gray songbird with an orange-pink underside. Its long, forked tail looks like a pair of scissors. The scissor-tailed flycatcher became Oklahoma's state bird in 1951.

*In 1990, Oklahoma chose an official game bird. This is the wild turkey. It lives in forests and **marshlands** throughout the eastern United States.*

The cardinal became Virginia's state bird in 1950. Cardinals travel very little. Most live their entire lives within a mile of where they were born. They build bowl-shaped nests in bushes and small trees.

Learning about Comparative Adjectives

Comparative adjectives compare nouns or pronouns. When adjectives are used to compare two nouns or pronouns, *er* is sometimes added. When they are used to compare three or more nouns or pronouns, *est* is sometimes added. In this sentence about the Mississippi magnolia, one of the adjectives will be changed to show this comparative form.

From May to June, this beautiful tree produces large, fragrant, white flowers.

The flowers in this tree are larger than those in the redbud.

Of all three trees, the magnolia has the largest flowers.

Other adjectives use *more* or *less* to compare two nouns or pronouns, and *most* or *least* to compare three or more nouns or pronouns. An example is shown using the adjective "beautiful" from the sentence about the magnolia.

This tree is more beautiful than the pine.

Of all three trees, the magnolia is the most beautiful.

Avoid using the *er* and *est* types with the *more* and *most*, or *less* and *least* types. For example, you would not say *more larger* or *most largest*.

Now, visit **www.usna.usda.gov/Gardens/collections/statetree flower.html**, and compare the magnolia to one of trees found on this site. Write down two adjectives that compare these trees.

Forming Comparative Adjectives

Read the paragraphs about Minnesota's common loon and Maine's black-capped chickadee. Some adjectives are shaded red. Write these adjectives in your notebook.

Minnesota chose the common loon as its state bird in 1961. These water birds are known for their four unique calls. The tremolo sounds like a crazy laugh. It can be used in greeting or to express worry. Mates use a soft wail to locate each other in the water. The yodel is a long, rising call that males use to defend their space. Family members use a soft hoot to find each other.

Maine chose its state bird in 1927. It is the black-capped chickadee. This plump, round songbird has white cheeks. The top of its head and its chin are black. Its wings are gray-green. The black-capped chickadee is one of the best-loved birds in North America.

Change the adjectives on this page into their comparative forms like the example shown below.

Adjective	Comparative
unique	more unique
soft	softer

Learning about Other Adjectives

Instead of describing or comparing, some adjectives point to particular nouns or pronouns. These adjectives tell *which* and *how many*. The example shows each type.

> This flag has nine stars.

Other adjectives called articles include *the, a*, and *an*. *The* is used to refer to a certain person, place, or thing. *A* and *an* refer to any person, place, or thing. These adjectives are shown in the following example.

> The flag shows an elk and a moose.

Articles and other adjectives that tell *which* and *how many* are shaded red in this paragraph about the state flag of Michigan.

Since becoming a state in 1837, there have been three state flags. The present flag has a coat of arms with an eagle holding an olive branch and arrows. The flag shows an elk and a moose supporting the coat of arms. It also depicts a man standing on a grassy peninsula. This flag became Michigan's official flag in 1911.

Now write this paragraph without the selected adjectives. Read it aloud. How does it sound without these adjectives?

Using Other Adjectives

In the paragraphs about the state flags of Minnesota and Oklahoma, some of the articles and other adjectives that tell *which* and *how many* have been replaced by black squares. Complete the paragraphs by including the missing articles and other adjectives that tell *which* and *how many*. Use the pictures to help you.

The first list should be used for the Minnesota state flag, and the second list for the Oklahoma state flag.

1. The   a   the   19

2. This   the   a   These   an   A   Seven

The first state flag of Minnesota was adopted in 1893 and designed by Mrs. Edward H. Center. A new flag was designed and adopted in 1957. ■ flag is royal blue, fringed in gold, and has ■ stars. The large star represents the North Star and Minnesota. There is ■ seal in ■ center of the flag. The French words, l'étoile du nord, which means "star of the north," are written in yellow letters on a red banner.

The current flag of Oklahoma is ■ state's 14th flag. ■ blue flag has ■ Native American war shield in the center. There are small crosses on the shield. ■ crosses are the Native American design for stars. ■ eagle feathers drop from the edge of the shield. ■ Native American peace pipe and ■ olive branch are together. Both are symbols of peace.

Where Do They Belong?

Now, you should be able to identify each type of adjective when it is used. In the paragraph about Montpelier, the state capital of Vermont, some adjectives have been shaded red.

Montpelier became Vermont's *state capital* in 1805. It has the *smallest population of all the state capitals.* More than 8,000 *people live in Montpelier. European settler, Colonel Jacob Davis, named this city after the French city, Montpelier.*

Each of the adjectives shown belongs to one of the types you learned in this book. The chart shows where each one belongs.

Articles	Descriptive	Comparative	*Which*	*How Many*
the	state, French, European	smallest	this	more than 8,000

Grouping Adjectives

There are some adjectives in these paragraphs about two state capitals, Phoenix in Arizona, and Lansing in Michigan. In your notebook, draw a chart like the one on this page. Then, place each adjective from these paragraphs in its proper column. Some examples have been done for you.

Phoenix has been the capital of Arizona since 1889. Phoenix is located in the southern part of Arizona and has a population of more than four million people. Of all the state capitals, it has the largest population.

In 1847, Lansing became the state capital of Michigan. This city became the place where Olds Motor Vehicle Company began in 1905. After that year, it became an industrial center. Today, more than 450,000 people live there. Its population is smaller than that of Phoenix.

Articles	Descriptive	Comparative	*Which*	*How Many*
a	state	largest	This	more than 450,000

Using Adjectives to Create Sentences

It is important to use adjectives to describe nouns and pronouns in clear and interesting ways. Adjectives can be used to create your own sentences about things around you.

Start by selecting the descriptive adjectives and their nouns from the following sentences in the paragraph about Alaska's state flower, the forget-me-not. The adjectives are shaded red, and the nouns are blue.

Alaska's state flower is the forget-me-not. This is a type of wildflower. The forget-me-not has five sky-blue petals with a white ring around a yellow center. The forget-me-not blooms during the summer. It has been Alaska's official flower since 1917.

Now, write three sentences about the forget-me-not using as many of the selected adjectives as you can. One has been done for you.

The forget-me-not is the official flower of Alaska.

Creating Your Own Sentences Using Types of Adjectives

Look at the image on this page. It shows important U.S. symbols.

*The large white house is the official residence of the president of the United States. The U.S. Capitol is a beautiful building and is the seat of the U.S. Congress in Washington, DC. The tall Washington Monument is an important national memorial honoring George Washington. The marble Lincoln Memorial is a **monument** dedicated to Abraham Lincoln. All four symbols are located in Washington, DC.*

Use the Internet, or visit the library to find more information about these U.S. symbols. Then, in your notebook, write one sentence about each symbol, using the types of adjectives explained in this book.

Tools for Learning about Adjectives

What did you learn? Look at the topics in the "Skills" column. Compare them to the page number in the "Page" column. Review the content you learned about adjectives by reading the "Content" column below.

SKILLS	CONTENT	PAGE
Defining an adjective	The South, Hawai'i's hibiscus	4–5
Identifying types of adjectives	Missouri's flowering dogwood, state seals of Ohio and Maine	6–7
Learning about descriptive adjectives	Minnesota red pine, state birds of Oklahoma and Virginia	8–9
Learning about comparative adjectives	Mississippi's magnolia, state birds of Minnesota and Maine	10–11
Learning about other adjectives	State capitals of Vermont, Arizona, and Michigan	12–13
Grouping adjectives according to type	Montpelier, Phoenix, and Lansing	14–15
Using adjectives	State flower of Alaska, image of White House, U.S. Capitol, and Lincoln Memorial	16–17

Practice Writing Your Own Paragraphs Using Different Types of Adjectives

These pictures show the state seals of Alaska and California. Study these state seals carefully. Then, make a list of all the adjectives you can use to describe what you see in these pictures. Write a paragraph about both state seals using these adjectives.

Put Your Knowledge to Use

Read these paragraphs about some symbols of New York, including its state tree, flower, and bird. There are many adjectives in these paragraphs. Use as many of these adjectives as you can to write a short story describing New York's three symbols.

New York's sugar maples grow in cold moist climates. Unlike other trees, they can grow in shady areas. Their winged seeds spin like helicopters as they fall from the tree. These trees can live for up to 400 years. They stop growing tall at about 150 years. After that, they only grow wider.

In 1890, New York's schoolchildren voted the rose as the state flower. The state government officially accepted the rose in 1955. A tea rose is most often used as New York's flower. Tea roses are large and have a spicy, tea-like smell.

*In 1928, New York's women chose the eastern bluebird to be the state bird. The New York government finally made this bird a state **emblem** in 1970. Eastern bluebirds are known for their many songs. They have different songs for courting a mate, protecting their space, and other activities.*

Use the Internet, or visit the library to find more information about the official symbols in a state of your choice. Try writing a paragraph describing three of those symbols using the types of adjectives that you learned in this book.

Then, write your own stories comparing your three symbols to three other symbols from another state. The following are symbols of Iowa. You can start with these.

Wild Rose

American Goldfinch

Iowa's Sate Seal

EXPANDED CHECKLIST

Reread your sentences, paragraphs, or stories to make sure that you have all of the following.

- ☑ Adjectives that describe size, color, or quality
- ☑ Adjectives that compare nouns or pronouns
- ☑ Adjectives that tell *which*
- ☑ Adjectives that tell *how many*
- ☑ Adjectives that are articles

Other Parts of Speech

You have now learned the tools for using adjectives. You can use your knowledge of adjectives to write clear and interesting descriptive sentences, paragraphs, or stories. There are four other parts of speech. You can use some of the same tools you learned in this book to use these other parts of speech. The chart below shows the other parts of speech and their key features.

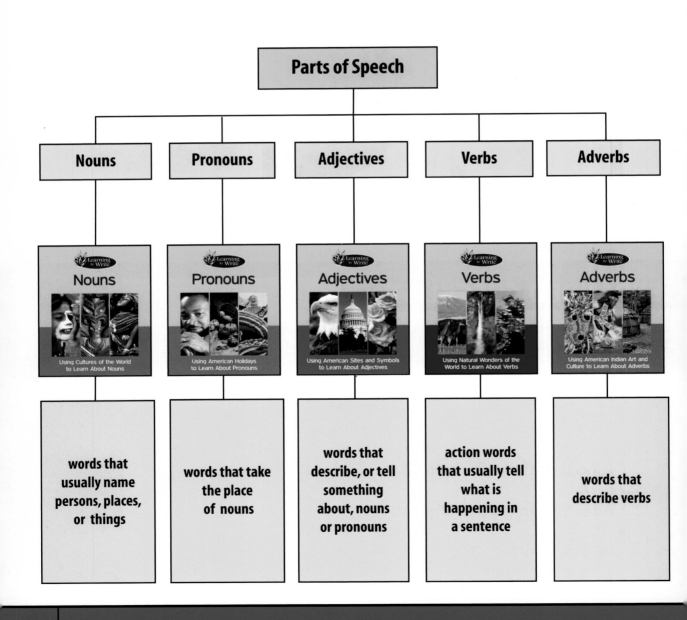

		Parts of Speech		
Nouns	**Pronouns**	**Adjectives**	**Verbs**	**Adverbs**
Nouns — Using Cultures of the World to Learn About Nouns	Pronouns — Using American Holidays to Learn About Pronouns	Adjectives — Using American Sites and Symbols to Learn About Adjectives	Verbs — Using Natural Wonders of the World to Learn About Verbs	Adverbs — Using American Indian Art and Culture to Learn About Adverbs
words that usually name persons, places, or things	words that take the place of nouns	words that describe, or tell something about, nouns or pronouns	action words that usually tell what is happening in a sentence	words that describe verbs

Further Research

Books

Many books provide information on adjectives. To learn more about how to use different types of adjectives, you can borrow books from the library. To learn more about U.S. sites and symbols, try reading these books.

Hurtig, Jennifer. *Capitals*. New York, NY: Weigl Publishers Inc., 2009.

Tait, Leia. *Birds*. New York, NY: Weigl Publishers Inc., 2009.

Watson, Galadriel. *Trees*. New York, NY: Weigl Publishers Inc., 2009.

Websites

On the Internet, you can type terms, such as "adjectives" or "types of adjectives," into the search bar of your Web browser, and click the search button. It will take you to a number of sites with this information.

Read more about the sites and symbols in all the American states at **www.infoplease.com/states.html** and **www.statesymbolsusa. org/index.html**.

Glossary

being verb: often called a linking verb because it links the subject of the sentence with information about it

emblem: an object that symbolizes something

endangered: animals whose populations are so low, they are in danger of disappearing completely

environment: the area in which a person, animal, or plant exists or lives

marshlands: areas or regions characterized by marshes or swamps

monument: a structure built in memory of a person or event, such as a building, pillar, or statue

noun: the part of speech that is usually used to name a person, place, or thing

pronoun: the part of speech that is used instead of a noun

seals: official symbols or marks

symbol: an object or idea that represents something other than itself

Index